TEAM BUILDING: AN EXERCISE IN LEADERSHIP

REVISED EDITION

Robert B. Maddux

CRISP PUBLICATIONS, INC.
Los Altos, California

TEAM BUILDING: AN EXERCISE IN LEADERSIHP

REVISED EDITION

CREDITS
Editor: **Michael Crisp**
Designer: **Carol Harris**
Typesetting: **Interface Studio**
Cover Design: **Carol Harris**
Artwork: **Ralph Mapson**

Library of Congress Catalog Card Number 86-70870
Maddux, Robert B.
Team Building: An Exercise in Leadership
ISBN O-931961-16-5

PREFACE

In all economic systems, people must produce the goods and services that are essential to life. How well, and how much they produce depends on their knowledge; skill; creativity; commitment; attitude; the technology employed; and finally the quality of those who manage them.

Typically, people work in small groups which have common or related functions. Each person in such a group has an individual aspiration, level of skill, and attitude toward the task. Since people think, feel and respond according to their individuality, they sometimes do not consider the benefits of supporting and cooperating with others to achieve a common goal. This can be seen at the first practice of any junior high school athletic team. Some players have considerable talent, others are less skillful. Ultimately the group will not have much success until they are motivated to work toward a common goal. A skilled coach will be able to pool their talent and train them to play together compensating for individual strengths and weaknesses.

Similarly, in a work environment, the results achieved are seldom the outcome of one individual's talent. Each person is influenced by the attitude and action of coworkers and managers. If the influence of the work environment is positive, a person tends to be productive. The same is true for a group of workers. When the influence is negative, both individuals and groups tend to be less productive.

This book is devoted to teaching concepts which make work positive and productive. It contains principles by which a group can be transformed into a team. The concepts are easily understood but their application takes dedication and effort. Good Luck!

Robert B. Maddux

ABOUT THIS BOOK

TEAM BUILDING: AN EXERCISE IN LEADERSHIP is not like most books. It has a unique ''self-paced'' format that encourages a reader to become personally involved. Designed to be ''read with a pencil'', there are an abundance of exercises, activities, assessments and cases that invite participation.

The objective of TEAM BUILDING is to help a person recognize the differences between groups and teams; and then make any required behavioral changes which apply concepts presented in the book to that person's unique management situation.

TEAM BUILDING (and the other self-improvement books listed on page 73) can be used effectively in a number of ways. Here are some possibilities:

— Individual Study. Because the book is self-instructional, all that is needed is a quiet place, some time and a pencil. By completing the activities and exercises, a person should not only receive valuable feedback, but also practical ideas about steps for self-improvement.

— Workshops and Seminars. The book is ideal for pre-assigned reading prior to a workshop or seminar. With the basics in hand, the quality of the participation should improve. More time can be spent on concept extensions and applications during the program. The book can also be effective when a trainer distributes it at the beginning of a session, and leads participants through the contents.

— Remote Location Training. Copies can be sent to those not able to attend ''home office'' training sessions.

— Informal Study Groups. Thanks to the format, brevity and low cost, this book is ideal for ''brown-bag'' or other informal group sessions.

There are other possibilities that depend on the objectives, program or ideas or the user. One thing for sure, even after it has been read, this book will serve as excellent reference material which can be easily reviewed.

CONTENTS

Preface	i
About This Book	iii
Which Objectives Do You Want To Achieve?	3
Groups Versus Teams	5
Group Managers Versus Team Leaders	7
Team Concepts Can Be Applied In Any Organization	9
What Can Team Building Do For Me?	11
Attitudes Of An Effective Team Builder	13
Case 1—Can This Supervisor Be Saved?	15
Become An Effective Planner	19
Strengthen Your Organizing Skills	21
Build A Motivating Climate	23
Establish A Control System	25
Case 2—Which Supervisor Would You Prefer?	27
Select Qualified People	29
Make Training Useful	31
Employee Focus And Commitment	33
Make Commitment Possible	35
Involve The Team In Setting Goals And Standards	37
Teach Employees Problem Solving Techniques	39
Conditions Which Support Team Problem Solving	41
Case 3—The Complaining Employees	43
Collaboration As A Source Of Power In Team Building	45
Facilitate Open Communication	47
Review Your Communication Skills	49
Understand Conflict	51
Case 4—Resolving Conflict	55
Building Trust	57
Use Praise Wisely	59
Accentuate The Positive	61
Reading Review	63
Ten Unforgivable Mistakes	65
Develop A Personal Action Plan	67
Voluntary Contract	69
Answers to Cases	70

SOME IMPORTANT OBJECTIVES FOR THE READER

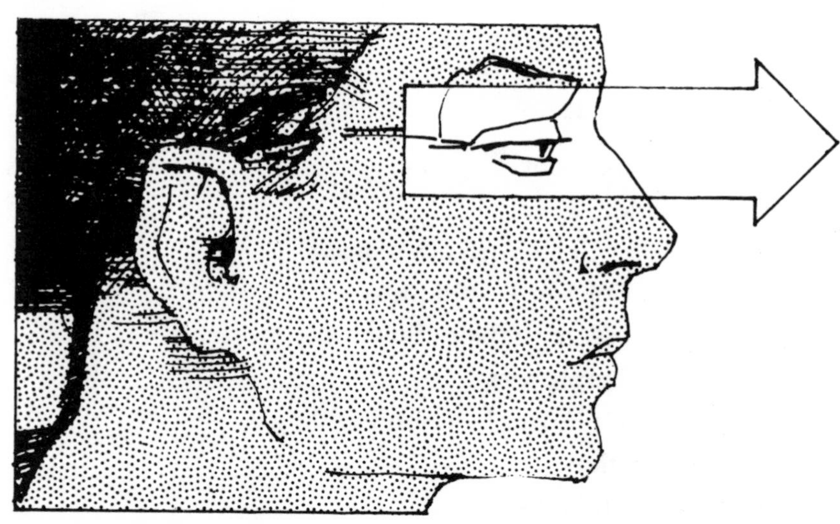

WHICH OBJECTIVES DO YOU WANT TO ACHIEVE

Objectives give us a sense of direction; a definition of what we plan to accomplish; and a sense of fulfillment when they are achieved. Check the objectives that are important to you. This book will help you achieve them.

I HOPE TO:

- ☐ Be able to explain the difference between a group and a team.
- ☐ Learn how to recognize situations that call for team rather than group behavior.
- ☐ Learn how to build a team from a group.
- ☐ Be able to understand and apply leadership techniques.
- ☐ Enjoy the personal and organizational rewards of team behavior.

GROUPS ARE FUNDAMENTAL UNITS OF ORGANIZATION

From the beginning of time people have formed groups. Groups provide the basis for family living, protection, waging war, government, recreation and work. Group behavior has ranged from total chaos to dramatic success, but it is increasingly evident that groups enjoy their greatest success when they become more productive units called teams.

Managers in many organizations seem content with group performance. This is often because they have not thought beyond what is being accomplished to what might be achieved under slightly different circumstances. Other leaders using the same number of people, doing similar tasks with the same technology somehow manage to improve productivity dramatically by establishing a climate where people are willing to give their best and work together in teams.

A comparison of teams and groups is shown on the facing page, check ☑ the characteristics representative of the unit of which you are currently a part.

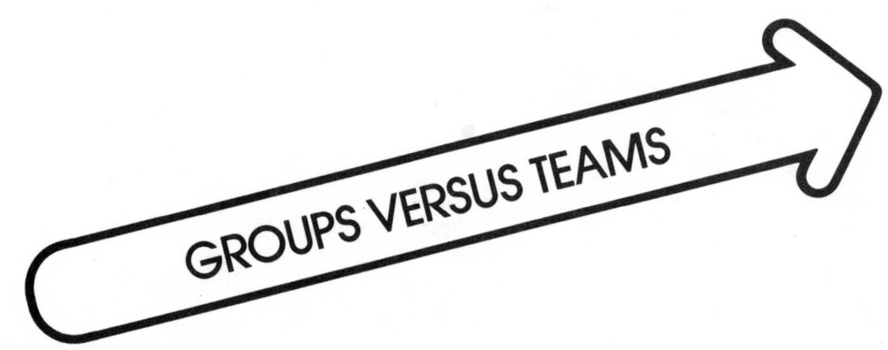

GROUPS	TEAMS
☐ Members think they are grouped together for administrative purposes only. Individuals work independently; sometimes at cross purposes with others.	☐ Members recognize their interdependence and understand both personal and team goals are best accomplished with mutual support. Time is not wasted struggling over "turf" or attempting personal gain at the expense of others.
☐ Members tend to focus on themselves because they are not sufficiently involved in planning the unit's objectives. They approach their job simply as a hired hand.	☐ Members feel a sense of ownership for their jobs and unit because they are committed to goals they helped establish.
☐ Members are told what to do rather than being asked what the best approach would be. Suggestions are not encouraged.	☐ Members contribute to the organization's success by applying their unique talent and knowledge to team objectives.
☐ Members distrust the motives of colleagues because they do not understand the role of other members. Expressions of opinion or disagreement are considered divisive or non-supportive.	☐ Members work in a climate of trust and are encouraged to openly express ideas, opinions, disagreements and feelings. Questions are welcomed.
☐ Members are so cautious about what they say that real understanding is not possible. Game playing may occur and communications traps be set to catch the unwary.	☐ Members practice open and honest communication. They make an effort to understand each other's point of view.
☐ Members may receive good training but are limited in applying it to the job by the supervisor or other group members.	☐ Members are encouraged to develop skills and apply what they learn on the job. They receive the support of the team.
☐ Members find themselves in conflict situations which they do not know how to resolve. Their supervisor may put off intervention until serious damage is done.	☐ Members recognize conflict is a normal aspect of human interaction but they view such situations as an opportunity for new ideas and creativity. They work to resolve conflict quickly and constructively.
☐ Members may or may not participate in decisions affecting the team. Conformity often appears more important than positive results.	☐ Members participate in decisions affecting the team but understand their leader must make a final ruling whenever the team cannot decide, or an emergency exists. Positive results, not conformity are the goal.

Team leaders exhibit different styles than those who are content managing a group. These styles are shaped by each person's life experience and the values they have adopted over the years.

Given today's rapid rate of organizational change, and the changing needs of people, it is important for those "in charge" to re-evaluate and modify their styles on a regular basis. This is the only way they can make the adaptations necessary to continue to be effective.

See how team centered leadership differs from group centered management on the facing page–then make a commitment to creating and supporting a team effort.

Plan you will make any needed changes in your style and evaluate the results carefully. Keep making adjustments until you achieve the results desired. Stay on the alert for additional ways to improve your leadership.

DIFFERENCES BETWEEN GROUP-CENTERED MANAGERS AND TEAM-CENTERED MANAGERS

Identify the qualities which best describe you at this time with a ☑.

GROUP CENTERED

☐ Overriding concern to meet current goals inhibits thought about what might be accomplished through reorganizing to enhance member contributions.

☐ Reactive to upper management, peers and employees. Find it easier to go along with the crowd.

☐ Willing to involve people in planning and problem solving to some extent but, within limits.

☐ Resents or distrusts employees who know their jobs better than the manager.

☐ Sees group problem solving as a waste of time, or an abdication of managerial responsibility.

☐ Controls information and communicates only what group members need or want to know.

☐ Ignores conflict between staff members or with other groups.

☐ Sometimes slow to recognize individual or group achievements.

☐ Sometimes modifies group agreements to suit personal convenience.

TEAM CENTERED

☐ Current goals are taken in stride. Can be a visionary about what the people can achieve as a team. Can share vision and act accordingly.

☐ Proactive in most relationships. Exhibits personal style. Can stimulate excitement and action. Inspires teamwork and mutual support.

☐ Can get people involved and committed. Makes it easy for others to see opportunities for teamwork. Allows people to perform.

☐ Looks for people who want to excel and can work constructively with others. Feels role is to encourage and facilitate this behavior.

☐ Considers problem solving the responsiblity of team members.

☐ Communicates fully and openly. Welcomes questions. Allows the team to do its' own filtering.

☐ Mediates conflict before it becomes destructive.

☐ Makes an effort to see that both individual and team accomplishments are recognized at the right time in an appropriate manner.

☐ Keeps commitments and expects the same in return.

INCREASED PRODUCTIVITY IS THE BY-PRODUCT OF TEAMWORK

When productive teams are compared with less productive groups, there are some important differences involving the application of team concepts. Here is an example:

A study was made of twenty coal mines operating in the same geologic structure, drawing from the same labor pool, and subject to the same governmental regulations. Productivity was measured in tons of coal produced per employee per shift.

The mine with the highest productivity delivered 242 tons per employee contrasted with the lowest which mined 58 tons per employee. The other mines were somewhere in between.

Conclusions from this study were summarized as follows: "The primary difference was the way in which company management worked with the employees. The most productive mine provided employees with significantly more individual responsibility and involvement in goal setting and problem solving."

TEAM BUILDING CONCEPTS CAN BE APPLIED IN ANY ORGANIZATION

A diverse group formed each year to compete in a sport is an excellent example of team building. Groups develop into ''teams'' when their common purpose is understood by all of the members. Within effective teams each member plays an assigned role using his or her talent to the best advantage. When the members integrate their skills to accentuate strengths and minimize weaknesses team objectives are usually achieved. When on the other hand groups play as individuals, they usually fail. Most wins or losses are the result of ''teamwork''. In sports, feedback is often immediate. If teamwork is lacking, good managers can identify where the problems are, and initiate corrective action in order to change things until the desired results are achieved.

Like their athletic counterparts, groups organized to perform business, community and governmental functions can achieve far more when they work as ''teams''. Unfortunately, many leaders fail to recognize and apply the same principles as they would coaching a sport. In a work organization they do not understand how to transform their group into a productive team. One reason may be that feedback in the form of results is not as quick or dramatic as in athletics. Problems can go unnoticed and corrective action if taken can be slow in coming.

Effective teamwork knows no level. It is just as important among top executives, as it is among middle managers, first line supervisors or the rank and file. The absence of teamwork at any level, (or between levels) will limit organizational effectiveness and can eventually kill an organization.

IT REQUIRES EFFORT TO ESTABLISH AND MAINTAIN TEAMWORK

If a leader does not place a high value on teamwork it will not occur. Teamwork takes conscious effort to develop and continuous effort to maintain, but the rewards can be great. Consider the examples on the facing page.

WHAT'S IN IT FOR ME?

WHAT CAN TEAM BUILDING DO FOR ME?

Leaders sometimes assign a low priority to team building because they have not considered the advantages that can accrue from a well executed team effort.

Following are some results of team performance. Check ☑ those you would like to achieve.

- ☐ Realistic, achievable goals can be established for the team and individual members because those responsible for doing the work contribute to their construction.
- ☐ Employees and leaders commit to support each other to make the team successful.
- ☐ Team members understand one another's priorities and help or support when difficulties arise.
- ☐ Communication is open. The expression of new ideas, improved work methods, articulation of problems and concerns is encouraged.
- ☐ Problem solving is more effective because the expertise of the team is available.
- ☐ Performance feedback is more meaningful because team members understand what is expected and can monitor their performance against expectations.
- ☐ Conflict is understood as normal and viewed as an opportunity to solve problems. Through open discussion it can be resolved before it becomes destructive.
- ☐ Balance is maintained between group productivity and the satisfaction of personal team members needs.
- ☐ The team is recognized for outstanding results, as are individuals for their personal contributions.
- ☐ Members are encouraged to test their abilities and try out ideas. This becomes infectious and stimulates individuals to become stronger performers.
- ☐ Team members recognize the importance of disciplined work habits and conform their behavior to meet team standards.
- ☐ Learning to work effectively as a team in one unit, is good preparation for working as a team with other units. It is also good preparation for advancement.

TEAMWORK AND PRODUCTIVITY GO HAND IN HAND

YOUR ATTITUDE WILL MAKE A BIG DIFFERENCE IN TEAM BUILDING

When the concept of team building is understood and applied at all levels in an organization it becomes much easier to transform groups into teams throughout the organization.

It is to any leader's advantage, however, to develop a team whether others are doing so or not. A positive attitude toward team building is essential.

Check your attitude by completing the exercise on the next page.

ATTITUDES OF AN EFFECTIVE TEAM BUILDER

The following attitudes support team building. This scale will help identify your strengths, and determine areas where improvement would be beneficial. Circle the number that best reflects where you fall on the scale. The higher the number, the more the characteristic describes you. When you have finished, total the numbers circled in the space provided.

1.	When I select employees I choose those who can meet the job requirements and work well with others.	7 6 5 4 3 2 1
2.	I give employees a sense of ownership by involving them in goal setting, problem solving and productivity improvement activities.	7 6 5 4 3 2 1
3.	I try to provide team spirit by encouraging people to work together and to support one another on activities that are related.	7 6 5 4 3 2 1
4.	I talk with people openly and honestly and encourage the same kind of communication in return.	7 6 5 4 3 2 1
5.	I keep agreements with my people because their trust is essential to my leadership.	7 6 5 4 3 2 1
6.	I help team members get to know each other so they can learn to trust, respect and appreciate individual talent and ability.	7 6 5 4 3 2 1
7.	I insure employees have the required training to do their job and know how it is to be applied.	7 6 5 4 3 2 1
8.	I understand that conflict within groups is normal, but work to resolve it quickly and fairly before it can become destructive.	7 6 5 4 3 2 1
9.	I believe people will perform as a team when they know what is expected, and what benefits will accrue.	7 6 5 4 3 2 1
10.	I am willing to replace members who can not or will not meet reasonable standards after appropriate coaching.	7 6 5 4 3 2 1

TOTAL ___________

A score between 60 and 70 indicates a positive attitude toward people and the type of attitude needed to build and maintain a strong team. A score between 40 and 59 is acceptable and with reasonable effort, team building should be possible for you. If you scored below 40, you need to carefully examine your attitude in light of current management philosophy.

APPROACH PEOPLE WITH RESPECT — TASKS WITH A CAN DO ATTITUDE!

Case studies help provide insights you may not already possess. Four case problems are included in this book. Please give each your careful attention.

The first case (on the opposite page) will help you understand the importance of learning and applying team building concepts.

CASE 1—CAN THIS SUPERVISOR BE SAVED?

Mary Lou has been supervisor to five employees for about three months. It is her first supervisory assignment, and she has had little training.

Although each employee has a different job with its' own standards, the tasks are interrelated and the success of the unit depends upon a cooperative effort. Mary Lou has worked hard to assign tasks, set deadlines and solve problems in order to achieve the desired results. The poor skills of two employees, and the constant bickering within the group however, has caused delays and personal frustration for everyone. Mary Lou would like to spend more time with her employees but paper work and reporting seem to consume most of her time. She also has begun to stay in her office more recently because of the hostility between the employees. Group productivity has fallen below expectations, and Mary Lou is increasingly afraid she may be fired.

What might Mary Lou do to save her job and turn the performance of the unit around?

____

____

____

____

____

____

____

CHECK YOUR ANSWER WITH THOSE OF THE AUTHOR ON PAGE 70.

TEAM BUILDING CAN BE COMPARED TO BASEBALL

- A skilled manager has responsibility to help select the players; coordinate the team's effort, and oversee the playing of the game.
- Players must know their jobs, have the skill to do them well, and be committed to make a contribution to the team.
- To beat the competition requires a game plan.
- Players and the manager must communicate with one another, trust and support one another, and resolve their differences in a constructive manner.
- Self-control must be exercised by each player, or in its absence, imposed by the manager.
- There must be a reward system that meets both the needs of the team and the personal needs of individual players.

COVER ALL THE BASES

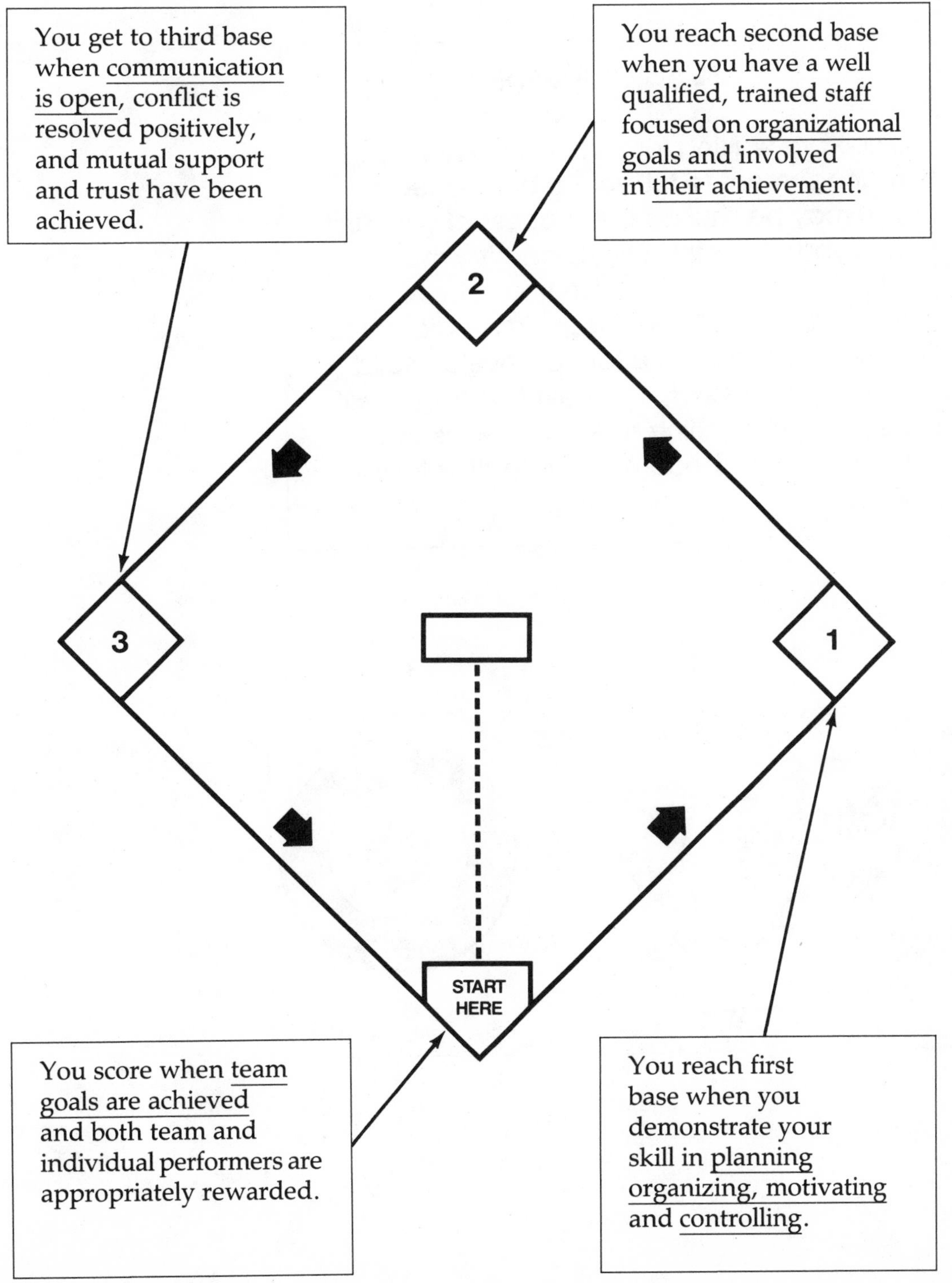

TIPS ON GETTING TO FIRST BASE

BE A SELF STARTER

If you are waiting for someone in higher management to tell you to build a team, you may be limiting the success of your unit and yourself. A thinking, proactive manager will not wait for a directive from above. Instead, he or she will begin immediately to make a concerted effort to develop solid management skills. The next few pages will help you determine how much work you have to do to become an effective team leader.

BECOME AN EFFECTIVE PLANNER

Teams need to know why they exist, what they are supposed to accomplish and who else is involved. If these areas are fuzzy, frustration is the result. Team members expect their leader to know the direction they are to take, and how they are to coordinate with other groups to reach their goals. To accomplish this, effective planning is required.

Planning is the thinking that precedes the work. If planning is not done, time and effort is usually wasted. Effective Planning includes the following elements. Check ☑ your proficiency level for each.

	Do Well	Should Improve
1. Interpreting goals which are passed down as the result of planning at higher levels.	☐	☐
2. Articulating organizational needs (including those of the team) into team goals and objectives.	☐	☐
3. Formulating implementation plans by examining alternatives and selecting activities which lead to successful results.	☐	☐
4. Identifying resources needed to achieve goals (people, time, money, materials and facilities) and insuring they are available.	☐	☐
5. Establishing time lines and completion target dates.	☐	☐
6. Determining standards of performance and how results will be measured.	☐	☐

Employees can make important contributions to planning once they become committed in the process. If you coordinate planning well, your team leadership will be much more effective. If you need to improve—DO IT NOW.

GOOD ORGANIZATIONAL SKILLS ARE ESSENTIAL TO REACH FIRST BASE

Leaders must be well organized and capable of helping the team organize itself to accomplish established goals.

One of the strengths of a good leader is the ability to see a future for the organization that is better in some important ways than what currently exists.

This view must then be communicated in such a way employees can organize their resources to achieve the desired results.

STRENGTHEN YOUR ORGANIZING SKILLS

Once planning is underway, organization becomes important. Resources—people, capital, raw materials, and technology, must be coordinated effectively to achieve team goals.

Team members look to the leader for direction and the allocation of resources. If organization is poor, the group will become confused, discouraged, argumentative, uncooperative and defensive. Teamwork will be impossible.

Some key aspects of organization are listed below. Check ☑ your proficiency in each.

	Do Well	Should Improve
1. I can divide work into logical tasks and groupings.	☐	☐
2. I know how to secure the resources required to achieve goals.	☐	☐
3. I am comfortable assigning tasks, resources and responsibility to team members on the basis of functions and skills.	☐	☐
4. I can establish guidelines in order to coordinate activities between team members and other groups involved with the outcome.	☐	☐
5. I make it a practice to design information systems which assure appropriate feedback as the work progresses.	☐	☐
6. I can establish communications networks to insure there is a free-flow of information up, down, and across organizational lines.	☐	☐

Employees can make important contributions to the organizing process because of their knowledge and experience. Employee involvement can enhance teamwork and efficiency. The better your organizational skills, the stronger you should be as a leader. If you need to improve—DO IT NOW!

MAKE AN EFFORT TO UNDERSTAND PEOPLE AND THEIR NEEDS

Establishing yourself as a strong leader requires an understanding of people and what motivates them. Those who understand can create a working climate in which team members can meet individual needs while achieving team goals.

Understanding what motivates individual employees requires time and effort but the results are worth it. The material on the next page will help you determine how good you are at buidling a climate which motivates employees to be successful.

BUILD A CLIMATE FOR MOTIVATION

People work for a variety of reasons. What is important for one person may have little significance to another. Motivation is personal and supervisors must get to know individual employees in order to learn what motivates them. Some people work for basic survival needs, while others are seeking security. Some work to fulfill ego satisfaction, or something even deeper.

A supervisor must be sensitive to recognize these employee needs, and design ways to meet them while achieving the goals of the organization. No single technique works for everyone. When the following elements are combined, however, both individual and team success is possible. Check ☑ your proficiency below.

I am proficient at:	Do Well	Should Improve
1. Insuring each employee knows what is expected and how performance will be measured.	☐	☐
2. Getting to know employees as individuals to learn their needs.	☐	☐
3. Providing the training and supervisory assistance necessary for each employee to achieve mutually established objectives.	☐	☐
4. Providing the resources required to perform the job.	☐	☐
5. Guiding and encouraging personal growth for individual employees.	☐	☐
6. Recognizing and rewarding good performance and correcting, or eliminating poor performance when it occurs.	☐	☐

Good leaders know how to build a motivating climate. If you need to improve—DO IT NOW!

CONTROL IS ESSENTIAL TO ACHIEVING GOALS

A supervisor, like a manager in baseball, must keep the game plan in mind. As the action progresses, modifying and adjusting this plan may be necessary to keep the team focused and on target. This process is called controlling. Check your approach to control on the facing page.

ESTABLISH A CONTROL SYSTEM THAT WILL ASSURE GOAL ACHIEVEMENT

Once a project has begun, a control system is needed to make sure it will progress according to plan, and the ultimate objective will be achieved. Controls should be established during the planning process, and be as simple as possible.

Once a control system is in place, the leader and the team can compare what is happening with what was expected. Based on the ongoing results, it may be necessary to revise the objective, modify the plan, reorganize, take some added motivational steps, or other appropriate action. Some important aspects of controlling are listed below. Indicate your proficiency with each by checking ☑ the appropriate box.

I normally:	Do Well	Should Improve
1. Establish control elements as part of the project plan.	☐	☐
2. Set up time schedules and check points to measure progress.	☐	☐
3. Encourage feedback from team members throughout the project.	☐	☐
4. Evaluate problems or deviations from plans, and then construct a new action plan which is timely and appropriate.	☐	☐
5. Adjust objectives, plans, resources or motivational factors as required to meet the organizational goals.	☐	☐
6. Communicate progress and plan changes to those who need to know.	☐	☐

> In a team situation, employees should, by virtue of their involvement, do much of the controlling. If you need to improve your skills in this area—DO IT NOW!

CONGRATULATIONS!
YOU'VE REACHED FIRST BASE!

The case study on the next page will give you a chance to apply what you have learned.

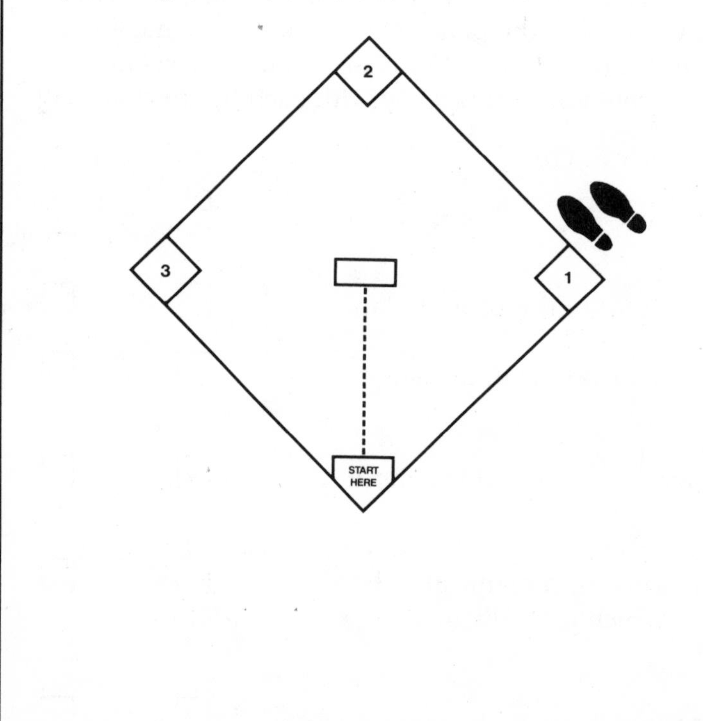

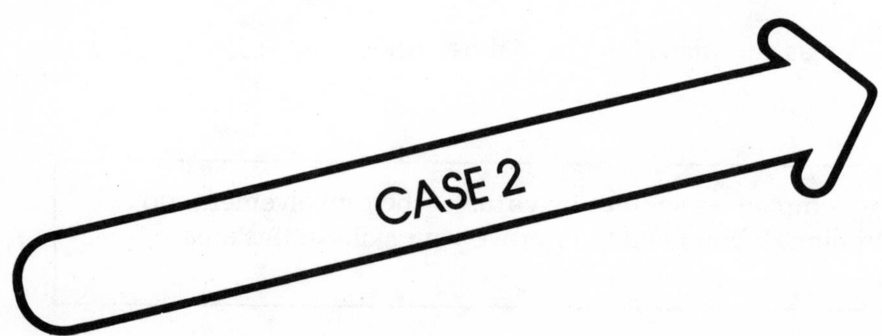

CASE 2—WHICH SUPERVISOR WOULD YOU PREFER?

Morgana and Jeff have just been promoted to their first supervisory position. Both have had considerable experience as Senior Micro-Technicians prior to the promotion. Morgana and Jeff shared plans for making the transition from technician to supervisor one day during lunch.

Morgana volunteered that she plans to concentrate on defining the work that needs to be done, and then provide her employees with precise goals and standards. Because of her experience and knowledge, she will also prepare a detailed performance plan for each employee. She feels this approach will ensure the goals are met while giving her the control she needs to get the job done.

Jeff responded by saying he had already secured his manager's agreement to take a supervisory skills course to insure he understood the management process. In the meantime, however, Jeff indicated he plans to involve his group in day to day planning, organizing and problem solving. Jeff is confident of his ability but feels every member of his staff is competent, and can make important contributions to the group's effectiveness. He also feels that individuals need the satisfaction that comes from being involved in a project.

Which of these supervisors would you rather work for? ____________________

____

____

____

Compare your response with the author's on page 70.

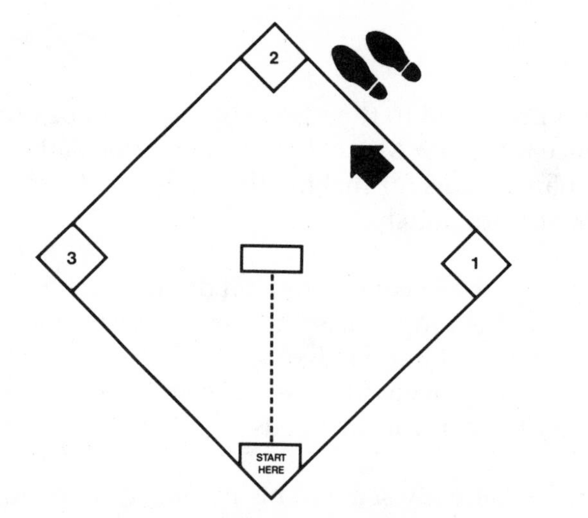

You are now on the way to second base. You will know you are there when you have a qualified trained staff that is focused on organizational goals and involved in their achievement.

SELECT QUALIFIED PEOPLE*

Human resources are the most critical part of any organization's success. Good people help insure profitability, productivity, growth and long term survival. You simply cannot survive without qualified people. As a team leader it is essential these people learn to work together. Some critical elements in employee selection and placement are listed below. Indicate how well you perform by checking ☑ the appropriate box.

	Do Well	Should Improve
1. I analyze job requirements thoroughly before beginning the selection process.	☐	☐
2. I always probe for objective evidence of an applicant's skills; knowledge; past successes and failures; dependability; and attitude toward work; co-workers; supervision and customers.	☐	☐
3. I describe my idea of teamwork to applicants and ask them to assess how they would work under team conditions.	☐	☐
4. I make sure each applicant understands the job requirements and expected standards of performance.	☐	☐
5. I evaluate facts carefully and avoid making premature conclusions or sterotyping while making a selection decision.	☐	☐
6. People I hire are placed in positions where there is potential for success.	☐	☐

NOTICE

If the people you select to be on your team are not successful, you will not be successful.

IF YOU NEED TO IMPROVE YOUR SELECTION AND PLACEMENT PRACTICES—DO IT NOW!

*For an excellent book on job interviews, order a copy of QUALITY INTERVIEWING. See order form on page 74.

WELL TRAINED EMPLOYEES MAKE MORE EFFECTIVE TEAM MEMBERS

Well trained employees have confidence in their ability to contribute to the team effort. They understand why it is important to help support other members of the team.

Resources such as knowledge of the needs of the organization; and control of work assignments are often available only to supervisors.

Any manager interested in improving team performance will insure training for each team member is appropriate.

The suggestions on the next page will help you assess your current attitude and approach toward training.

MAKE TRAINING USEFUL

Are you an effective trainer? Your attitude, knowledge and approach will influence what is learned and how well it is applied. Here are some suggestions to improve the return on investment in training for all concerned.

Place a ☑ if you already do what is suggested and an ☒ if you plan to begin this practice.

I normally:

☐ 1. Review performance against expectations with each employee periodically, and jointly identify training that will strengthen results.

☐ 2. Listen to an employee's growth objectives, and support them when it is appropriate to do so.

☐ 3. Talk in advance to employees selected for training to reinforce the importance of the training to their job.

☐ 4. Have an employee's work covered by others while they are in training so they can concentrate on what is being taught.

☐ 5. Help employees develop an action plan to apply their training to the job.

☐ 6. Ask the employee for an evaluation of the training program and whether it would be suitable for other members of the team.

☐ 7. Assign work to employees that allows them to apply new techniques and methods learned during training.

☐ 8. Compliment employees when they apply their newly acquired skills.

SECOND BASE IS JUST STEPS AWAY WHEN TEAM MEMBERS UNDERSTAND AND COMMIT TO ORGANIZATIONAL GOALS.

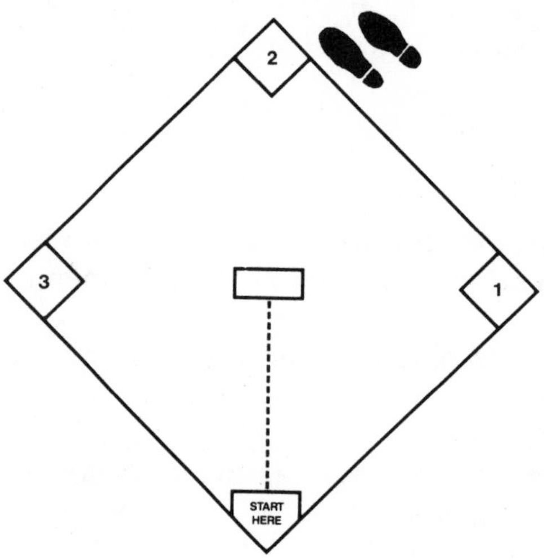

Your management style can help focus employee efforts to achieve organizational goals.

The next page describes 3 different approaches to management. Which best fits you?

EMPLOYEE FOCUS AND COMMITMENT IS INFLUENCED BY MANAGEMENT STYLE

☐ **"I know best."**—This person feels work should be done by controlling the people who do it. Employees are told what to do, how to do it, and when to stop. Then they are told what they did wrong and what they did right; where they are weak, and where they are strong. The person in charge feels this is justified because of his or her superior knowledge and ability. This attitude does not invite new ideas, challenge people, or stimulate a cooperative, supportive spirit. Communication is directed one way only.

☐ **"I'll set the goals, you meet them."**—This person feels that because of his or her superior knowledge, ability or experience it is O.K. to establish goals for others to meet. The employee is given an opportunity to discuss ways to meet goals, but has no input into the actual performance objectives. When this happens commitment is more difficult to obtain from employees because their lack of involvement precludes a sense of ownership.

☐ **"Let's review the work together, establish more realistic goals and evaluate performance accordingly."**—This leader emphasizes work performance, not authoritarian control. The idea is to first communicate organizational needs, then help team members contribute their ideas. The leader acts as a resource and enabler rather than as a judge. Communication is open and flows in both directions. The value of mutual support and cooperation is recognized and employed.

DID YOU CHECK ☑ THE ONE MOST LIKE YOU?

TEAM MEMBERS MUST BE COMMITTED

Supervisors cannot do it all, no matter how talented and committed they may be. Their success is measured by the ability to delegate intelligently and then motivate employees to accomplish the goals of the organization. The highest level of achievement is attained when a team is committed to the task, and full use is made of each member's talents.

MAKE COMMITMENT POSSIBLE

Commitment cannot be forced. It is self-generating and usually develops through a feeling of involvement. People increase commitment to a team when they are allowed to contribute to its success. Once actively involved in goal setting and problem solving, a sense of ownership is developed. Team goals can be effectively pursued, much like an entrepreneur. Employees feel more important (and needed) when they feel a responsibility for results. This is the time a genuine concern is developed for other team members. Group problems become individual problems, and team goals become individual goals. Members contribute their best to problem-solving because they have a personal stake in doing so.

When members help design the systems and methods used by the team, they understand why controls are important and make a commitment to support them. This is especially true when they know it is possible to revise or improve controls when required.

Involvement also helps team members satisfy the participative needs of others. It helps build a framework in which individual member needs can be learned, understood and supported by all.

A supervisor controls the degree to which employees are involved. Open up opportunities for participation and watch the commitment grow.

INVOLVE TEAM MEMBERS INDIVIDUALLY AND CORPORATELY IN SETTING GOALS AND STANDARDS

A **goal** is a statement of results to be achieved. Goals describe: (1) conditions that will exist when the desired outcome has been accomplished; (2) a time frame during which the outcome is to be completed; and (3) resources the organization is willing to commit to achieve the desired result.

A **standard** refers to an ongoing performance criteria that must be met time and again. Standards are usually expressed quantitatively, and refer to such things as attendance, breakage, manufacturing tolerances, production rates and safety standards.

Goals and standards should be challenging, but achievable. They should be established with the participation of those responsible for meeting them. After all, well selected, trained employees should know more about what is achievable than anyone else.

See the next page for some "how to" suggestions.

INVOLVE THE TEAM IN SETTING GOALS AND STANDARDS

Here is one way team members can help establish goals and standards and the action plans necessary to achieve them. Like other critical skills, goal setting may take practice.

The role of the team member and the leader are outlined below. Check ☑ those concepts with which you agree and are willing to try.

TEAM MEMBER	LEADER
☐ Helps establish performance goals and standards. This is a ''self-contract'' for achievement as well as a commitment to deliver a result for the team.	☐ Ensures team goals are achievable, but challenging enough to meet organizational needs and provide a sense of accomplishment
☐ Develops methods to measure results, and checkpoints for control purposes.	☐ Helps balance the complexity of measures and controls with value received.
☐ Outlines the action required to accomplish goals and standards.	☐ Participates with the team to test the action plan's validity against other alternatives.
☐ Specifies participation required from colleagues or in other units within the organization.	☐ Reviews what cooperation and support is required and helps obtain it if required.
☐ Reports progress as work is performed. Seeks guidance and assistance when needed. Adjusts plan as required.	☐ Follows the progress of the work. Reinforces achievement and assists in problem solving when indicated. Ensures targets are met, or modified if circumstances so indicate.

These roles place the responsibility for performance on the appropriate team members, and provides the latitude to achieve results. The leader concentrates on being a challenger, prober, coach and enabler.

GETTING EMPLOYEES INVOLVED MEANS PASSING ALONG OWNERSHIP OF PROBLEMS WHICH RIGHTFULLY BELONG TO THEM

Many supervisors spend too much time solving problems that could be better handled by individuals. When supervisors feel responsible for solving all the problems, production is slowed; employees are frustrated; and personal growth is limited. The supervisor ends up with less time to plan, organize, motivate and control.

Team effectiveness is more easily achieved when the supervisor simply participates in problem solving rather than dominating it.

TEACH PROBLEM SOLVING TECHNIQUES

Problem solving should be taught at every level of an organization. The process should be as simple as is required to get the job done. One basic approach is outlined below. Check ☑ those steps that would be useful in your operation.

☐ **Step 1—State what appears to be the problem.**
The real problem may not surface until facts have been gathered and analyzed. Therefore, start with a supposition that can later be confirmed or corrected.

☐ **Step 2—Gather facts, feelings and opinions.**
What happened? Where, when and how did it occur? What is its' size, scope, and severity? Who and what is affected? Is it likely to happen again? Does it need to be corrected? Time and expense may require problem solvers to think through what they need, and assign priorities to the more critical elements.

☐ **Step 3—Restate the problem.**
The facts help make this possible, and provide supporting data. The actual problem may, or may not be the same as stated in step 1.

☐ **Step 4—Identify alternative solutions.**
Generate ideas. Do not eliminate any possible solutions until several have been discussed.

☐ **Step 5—Evaluate alternatives.**
Which will provide the optimum solution? What are the risks? Are costs in keeping with the benefits? Will the solution create new problems?

☐ **Step 6—Implement the decision.**
Who must be involved? To what extent? How, when and where? Who will the decision impact? What might go wrong? How will results be reported and verified?

☐ **Step 7—Evaluate the results.**
Test the solution against the desired results. Modify the solution if better results are needed.

USE GROUP PROBLEM SOLVING TECHNIQUES WHEN SEVERAL INPUTS ARE NEEDED.

When a baseball player is not hitting properly, or making too many errors, it may be beneficial to seek the help of other professionals. Help may be requested by the player, come from a teammate, or the manager. Similar situations occur in other organizations. When they do, group interactions may be a solution. The degree of success obtained will depend on the effectiveness of the process used.

Some conditions that support effective team problem solving are listed on the next page.

CONDITIONS WHICH SUPPORT EFFECTIVE PROBLEM SOLVING BY TEAMS

Improved results can be obtained from a team involved in problem solving techniques when sound group processes are used. Team members commit to help find the best possible solution to a problem rather than impose their exclusive view. The leader participates as a team member and is subject to the same rules. Open communication is expected, and team members are encouraged to challenge ideas in order to test their usefulness to solve the problem. A successful solution from a group is often far more effective than single solutions offered by individuals. The following conditions support good team problem solving. Check ☑ those now existing in your team and place an ☒ by those you want to add in the future.

☐ 1. Team members readily contribute from their experience and *listen* to the contributions of others.

☐ 2. Conflicts arising from different points of view are considered helpful and are resolved constructively by the team.

☐ 3. Team members challenge suggestions they believe are unsupported by facts or logic, but avoid arguing just to have their way.

☐ 4. Poor solutions are not supported just for the sake of harmony or agreement.

☐ 5. Differences of opinion are discussed and resolved. Coin tossing, averaging, majority vote and similar cop-outs are avoided when making a decision.

☐ 6. Every team member strives to make the problem solving process efficient and is careful to facilitate rather than hinder discussion.

☐ 7. Team members encourage and support co-workers who may be reluctant to offer ideas.

☐ 8. Team members understand the value of time and work at eliminating extraneous and/or repetitious discussion.

☐ 9. Team decisions are not arbitrarily over-ruled by the leader simply because he/she does not agree with them.

☐ 10. The team understands the leader will make the best decision he or she can, if a satisfactory team solution is not forthcoming.

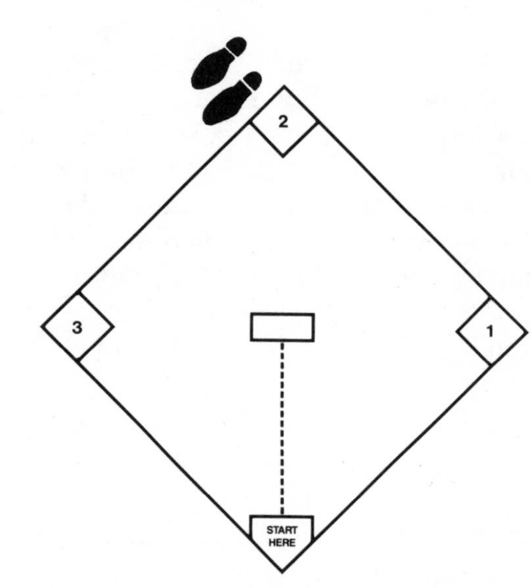

CONGRATULATIONS–YOU HAVE REACHED SECOND BASE!

Before heading for third, complete the case study on the facing page.

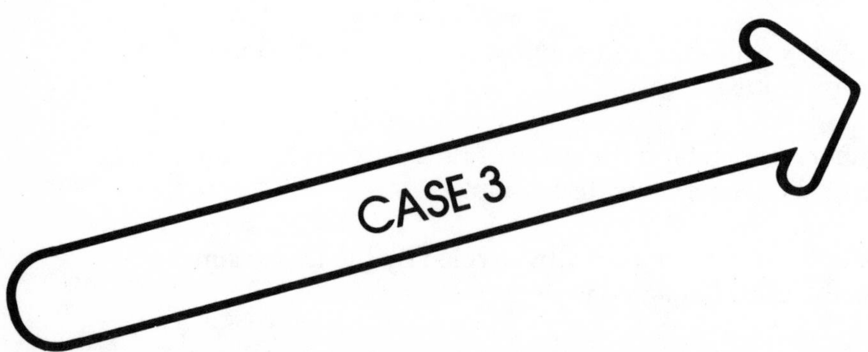

CASE 3—THE COMPLAINING EMPLOYEES

Joyce and Sue work in computer services under the supervision of Janice Johns. They are both depressed about their jobs and have been complaining to one another. Joyce is unhappy because she has never seen a description of her job and has only a limited understanding of what is expected of her. When she asked Janice about it, she was told, ''Don't worry , I'll keep you busy.'' Joyce never receives a new assignment until she completes the previous one she was assigned. Sometimes a day or more will pass before Janice is able to give Joyce a new project. Recently Joyce starting helping a co-worker because she had nothing else to do. Janice later told her: ''Don't do that again. Assignment of the work is my responsibility.'' Joyce has since been criticized by her co-workers for not pitching in when they are busy and she is not.

Sue, on the other hand, is concerned about the back-log building up in her job. The problem occurred because of repeated changes in project objectives which were not communicated until after a critical point in the work affected had been passed. Janice insists on personally handling all communications with other groups serviced by their department. Because Janice is so busy, she frequently fails to pass important information along to Sue and is equally slow in getting answers from Sue which are needed by others.

Are Sue's and Joyce's complaints justified? Yes ___ No ___
Support your position: ____

____

____

See page 71 for the author's ideas.

MAKING YOUR MOVE TO THIRD BASE

Once you have a qualified staff, properly trained and focused on organizational goals, you have accomplished a great deal, but you still have not reached home plate.

You must concentrate on building an atmosphere conducive to open communication, cooperation and trust not only within your team, but also between your team and other units of the organization.

Bringing team members together to collaborate on projects of mutual interest, and to generate ideas and suggestions for improvement of productivity is one way to do this.

COLLABORATION AS A SOURCE OF POWER IN TEAM BUILDING

Collaboration has many benefits when it is used well. In the list below, check ☑ those advantages of importance to you.

☐ Collaboration builds an awareness of interdependence. When people recognize the benefits of helping one another, and realize it is expected, they will work together to achieve common goals. The effort is non-threatening.

☐ When people work together to achieve common goals they stimulate each other to higher levels of accomplishment. Fresh ideas are generated and tested, and the team's productivity exceeds any combined efforts of employees working individually.

☐ Collaboration builds and reinforces recognition and mutual support within a team. People have an opportunity to see the effect of their effort and the efforts of others on achievement.

☐ Collaboration leads to commitment to support and accomplish organizational goals. People gain personal power in the form of confidence when they know others share their views and are acting in concert with them.

The benefits of collaboration make it easy to understand why managers who can make it happen are considered leaders. Collaboration can be encouraged and supported in the following ways. Check ☑ those you plan to use.

☐ Identify areas of interdependence that make collaboration appropriate. Involve team members in planning and problem solving to help them identify where collaboration is needed.

☐ Keep lines of communication open between everyone involved in a problem, project or course of action.

☐ Let the team know in advance that teamwork will positively influence individual recognition.

YOU MUST HAVE OPEN COMMUNICATION TO REACH THIRD BASE

A leader uses communication to gather, process and transmit information essential to the well being of the organization. Since this communication moves in many directions, leaders must carefully consider the needs of peers, superiors and team members.

The diagram on the next page reflects some important communication needs. If they are not met, team results will suffer.

FACILITATE OPEN COMMUNICATION

The team leader can often facilitate communications by responding to the information needs of the organization. Here are some typical examples.

What information do I need from above?

Where should I get it?

When should I get it?

What information should I pass up to my superiors?

How should it be conveyed?

How often is is required?

When should I send it?

What groups can provide specific information on policy and procedure?

How do I get it?

What do they expect from me?

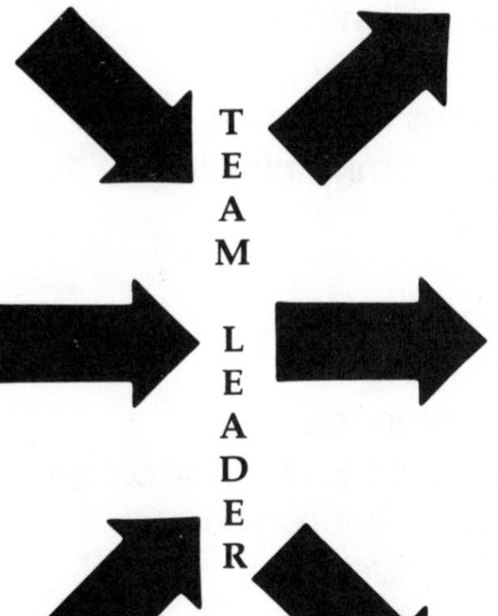

What groups depend on me for information?

Who do I give the information to?

When do I give them information?

How do I provide the information?

What information should I get from people working for me?

How should I get it?

How often?

What should I do with it?

What do employees working for me want to know?

How do I provide it?

When do I get someone else to provide it?

SENDING AND LISTENING SKILLS ARE ESSENTIAL TO GOOD COMMUNICATION

A player at second base must stay alert for a signal from the coach that it is safe to run to third. The clarity with which this signal is sent may make the difference between winning and losing.

Research shows the best leaders are good communicators. They have learned to give clear instructions; stay responsive to questions and suggestions; and keep the appropriate parties well informed.

Research also confirms a positive correlation between communication (understanding) and:

–improved productivity
–better problem solving
–a reduction in grievances
–ideas for improvement in methodology
–improved working relationships
–greater personal satisfaction

REVIEW YOUR COMMUNICATION SKILLS

REVIEW YOUR COMMUNICATIONS SKILLS

Complete each of the following statements by circling the most appropriate choice.

1. Messages are the most easily understood when:
   (a) you use your full command of the language.
   (b) they are sent in terms the receiver understands.

2. Complex information is more easily understood when you:
   (a) improve clarity by using specific examples and analogies.
   (b) tell the listener to pay careful attention.

3. Key concepts are better remembered when you:
   (a) use repetition to reinforce them.
   (b) express yourself clearly.

4. Organizing a message before transmitting it:
   (a) often takes more time than it is worth.
   (b) makes it easier to understand.

5. The sender can determine the receiver's understanding by:
   (a) asking if he or she understands.
   (b) asking the receiver to report what he or she heard.

6. Listening is more effective when you:
   (a) concentrate on the sender and what is being said.
   (b) anticipate what the speaker is going to say.

7. Understanding is easier when you:
   (a) suspend judgement until the sender finishes the message.
   (b) assume you know the senders position and judge accordingly.

8. Understanding can be improved by the listener:
   (a) periodically paraphrasing the message back to the sender.
   (b) interrupting to express feelings and emotions.

9. Good listeners:
   (a) have their response ready when the sender stops talking.
   (b) ask questions when they don't understand.

10. Sending and receiving are both enhanced when:
    (a) the parties maintain good eye contact.
    (b) the parties are defensive and challenge one another.

> Encourage team members to review communications skills using this same exercise. Then compare notes and discuss how to improve. This will be another cooperative step in building a stronger team effort.

ANSWERS: 1(b); 2(a); 3(a); 4(b); 5(b); 6(a); 7(a); 8(a); 9(b); 10 (a).

CONFLICT WITHIN ORGANIZATIONS IS INEVITABLE

In baseball, if two runners try to occupy the same base at the same time, there is conflict. It is an exicting situation, but if a positive solution is not found quickly, both they and their team will be losers.

Team leaders must accept the fact that any time two or more people are brought together, the stage is set for potential conflict. When conflict does occur, the results may be positive or negative depending upon how those involved choose to approach it.

With this in mind, team leaders must be sensitive to the fact that positive contributions can arise from conflict providing things do not get out of control. Teaching team members to understand conflict and resolve it positively will help the team succeed. The next few pages offer some tips on conflict management.

MAKE UNDERSTANDING THE NATURE OF CONFLICT A TEAM PROJECT

Some members of Memorial church want to use church funds to aid the local poor. Others prefer spending more money for missionary work. Still others think new carpeting for the sanctuary is the greatest need.

A sales manager wants a large inventory of all products so quick deliveries to customers can be promised. The manufacturing manager wants to limit the inventory to hold down storage costs.

In both of these situations everyone means well, and if questioned would maintain they were trying to accomplish what they perceive to be the best objective. Nonetheless, conflict is present because of:

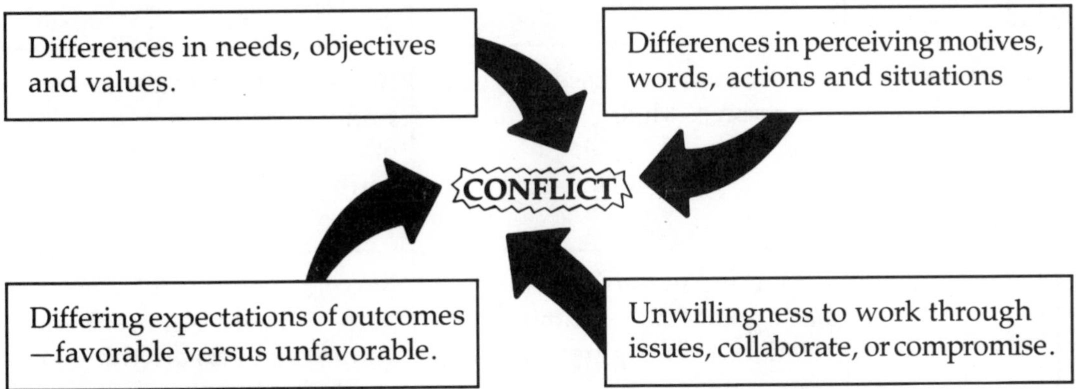

Conflict becomes unhealthy when it is avoided or approached on a win/lose basis. Animosities will develop, communications will break down, trust and mutual support will deteriorate, and hostilities will result. When sides are chosen productivity will diminsh or stop. The damage is usually difficult (sometimes impossible) to repair.

Conflict is healthy when it causes the parties to explore new ideas, test their position and beliefs, and stretch their imagination. When conflict is dealt with constructively, people can be stimulated to greater creativity, which will lead to a wider variety of alternatives and better results.

CONFLICT RESOLUTION STYLES

There are 5 basic approaches to conflict resolution. They can be summarized as follows. Indicate the one you are most likely to use with followers with an [F] ; your peers a [P] ; and with your supervisor a [S] .

STYLE	CHARACTERISTIC BEHAVIOR	USER JUSTIFICATION
Avoidance ☐ ☐ ☐	Non confrontational. Ignores or passes over issues. Denies issues are a problem.	Differences too minor or too great to resolve. Attempts might damage relationships or create even greater problems.
Accomodating ☐ ☐ ☐	Agreeable, non-assertive behavior. Cooperative even at the expense of personal goals.	Not worth risking damage to relationships or general disharmony.
Win/Lose ☐ ☐ ☐	Confrontational, assertive and aggressive. Must win at any cost.	Survival of the fittest. Must prove superiority. Most ethically or professionally correct.
Compromising ☐ ☐ ☐	Important all parties achieve basic goals and maintain good relationships. Aggressive but cooperative.	No one person or idea is perfect. There is more than one good way to do anything. You must give to get.
Problem Solving ☐ ☐ ☐	Needs of both parties are legitimate and important. High respect for mutual support. Assertive and cooperative.	When parties will openly discuss issues, a mutually beneficial solution can be found without anyone making a major concession.

Review this chart with team members. Share the answers to test each other's perceptions. Discuss ways conflicts can be more effectively resolved in the team and with other units.

You and your team may find the following diagram helpful in discussing conflict resolution styles.

Answer the following questions:

1. Which style is the most uncooperative and least assertive? ________________ .
2. Which style is characterized by assertive behavior, yet represents the maximum in cooperation? ________________ .
3. Which style is totally cooperative but unassertive? ________________ .
4. Which style is totally assertive and uncooperative? ________________ .
5. Which style takes the middle ground on assertiveness and cooperation? ______ .

Answers to questions 1 through 5: 1. Avoidance; 2. Problem Solving; 3. Accomodating; 4. Win/lose; 5. Compromising.

CASE 4

When team members understand the nature of conflict and constructive methods to resolve it, they can usually work out disagreements themselves. When they can't, or when the problem requires your intervention for other reasons, you may have to engineer a solution.

Test your skill at this by solving the case on the next page.

CASE 4—RESOLVING CONFLICT

Justin is supervisor of a small group of quality control testers in a chemical products laboratory. At different times, two testers have come to him with different suggestions for reporting test results to plant operations. The first, Jeremy wants to send the results to the foreman in charge of the unit where the samples were produced. Ginny on the other hand wants to send the reports directly to the lead operator on the unit so corrective changes can be made as soon as possible. Ginny and Jeremy are both good people but very competitive. Justin is aware they have already exchanged a few sharp remarks over the issue. Both ideas are reasonable and either is better than the current practice of sending reports to the administrative office.

In the choices below, identify the five basic approaches to conflict resolution in the blank provided. Then indicate with a check ☑ the approach you would use if you were Justin.

☐ 1. __________ Study the situation independently, decide who is right, and tell Jeremy and Ginny to implement your decision.

☐ 2. __________ Wait to see what happens.

☐ 3. __________ Let each handle their reporting their way.

☐ 4. __________ Get Jeremy and Ginny together to work out a solution they can both live with even though they must both give a little.

☐ 5. __________ Suggest Jeremy and Ginny combine their ideas so that both can achieve their goals, (send the report to the foreman with a copy to the lead operator).

Compare your answers with those of the author on page 71.

FINAL WORDS TO HELP YOU TO THIRD BASE

As people work through the team building processes, they get to know one another. They learn to respect individual differences; appreciate team contributions and enjoy the satisfaction teamwork provides when both personal and organizational goals are achieved.

Trust is an essential part of this experience. It is important because of the powerful effect it has on every aspect of team performance.

Over the years, the author of this book has asked participants in workshops to collaborate in writing down their feelings about trust. A few are shared on the following page.

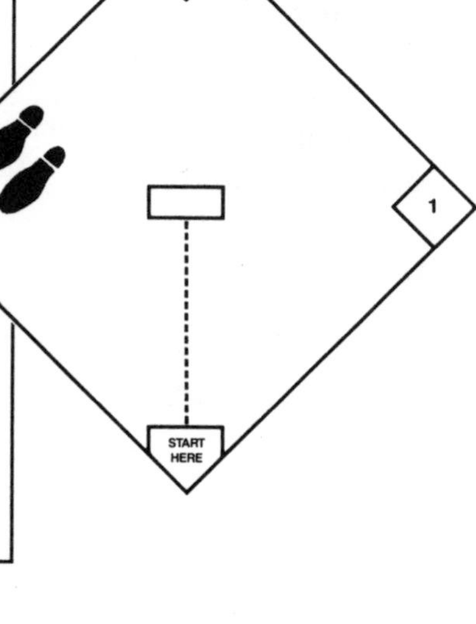

BUILDING TRUST IN TEAMS

The following trust statements are actual responses of individuals who learned team building techniques.

INDIVIDUAL	
A	To build trust it is essential to have clearly and consistently administered goals which contain employee input. Employees must perceive their managers as open, fair, honest and willing to listen. Managers must be decisive and stand by their decisions in difficult situations. Employees must have the confidence that their manager will support them, even in delicate matters, and take responsibility for group actions. A manager must also readily give credit to employees where credit is due.
B	I define trust as an assured reliance on the character, ability, and strength or truth of someone or something. Trust is built in a work group by promoting open communications; providing fair leadership and supervising with sensitivity.
C	Establishing trust in a work group requires open and honest communication, accepting others, sharing a common goal, and respecting the opinions of others on how to achieve that goal.
D	Trust is necessary to have a productive working environment. It is essential for all personnel to practice open, honest communication in order to increase awareness and build cooperation. This environment of trust promotes loyalty and commitment to achieve the goals and objectives of the organization.

When communications are open, conflict is resolved positively, and mutual support and trust have been achieved, you have rounded third base and are headed for home plate.

YOU SCORE WHEN TEAM GOALS ARE ACHIEVED AND TEAM PERFORMANCE IS APPROPRIATELY RECOGNIZED.

There are many forms of recognition, but one of the most powerful is praise. Some managers use praise effectively, others use it poorly or not at all. See the next page for some successes and failures.

WHICH WILL YOU BE?

SUCCESSES	FAILURES
Leaders who think it important to help people feel good about themselves.	Those who are insensitive to the needs of others.
Leaders who give periodic praise to team members for meeting job requirements	Those who think praise is improper for persons who meet, but do not exceed, job requirements.
Leaders who understand people respond better from praise of what they do well than by criticism of what they do wrong.	Those who only look for what is being done wrong and consistently give only negative feedback.
Leaders who give sincere praise for reasons the receiver can understand.	Those who are insincere and only use praise to get something they want.
Leaders who praise teamwork but also recognize individual contributions to final results.	Those who do not go to the trouble to reward teamwork or identify individual contributions.
Add from your own experience:	Add from your own experience:
____________________	____________________
____________________	____________________
____________________	____________________
____________________	____________________

PRAISE GIVEN WHEN EARNED REWARDS THE GIVER AS WELL AS THE RECEIVER.

BALL PLAYERS OFTEN CALL A TIME OUT TO GET FEEDBACK ON HOW THEY ARE DOING. ANY TEAM CAN PROFIT BY DOING THE SAME.

Team performance can be improved when members provide feedback on how well things are being done. Positive recognition when things are done right encourages similar performance in the future. Corrective action to re-direct inappropriate or inadequate performance clears the air and can set the stage for future success.

You have just reviewed some positive approaches to praise. On the facing page see how corrective action can also be taken using positive methods.

ACCENTUATE THE POSITIVE

Discipline is a basic requirement of team performance. A good leader maintains control but strives to establish an environment in which team members will exercise self-control. This is accomplished by following through on the true meaning of discipline, namely, ''training that develops or molds by instruction or exercise.'' The means by which positive discipline can be implemented are listed below. Indicate your proficiency with each technique by checking ☑ the appropriate box.

TECHNIQUE	DO WELL	SHOULD IMPROVE
1. From the outset, make sure team members understand what is expected of them and what standards are to be met.	☐	☐
2. Teach team members how to fulfill expectations and achieve standards.	☐	☐
3. Encourage team members as they make progress toward attaining company goals.	☐	☐
4. Compliment team members when standards are achieved and expectations are realized.	☐	☐
5. Re-direct inadequate or inappropriate performance when it occurs, and repeat 1-4.	☐	☐
6. If the inadequate or inappropriate performance persists after a reasonable period of time (and step 5 has been applied), bench or trade the player. He or she hasn't made the team.	☐	☐

This process, when consistently applied and followed, will eliminate most disciplinary problems. If you have not been doing this, you can institute it immediately with your entire team. Most people want to do the right thing but they often need guidance to know what that is.

CONGRATULATIONS!

You have rounded the bases in good form.

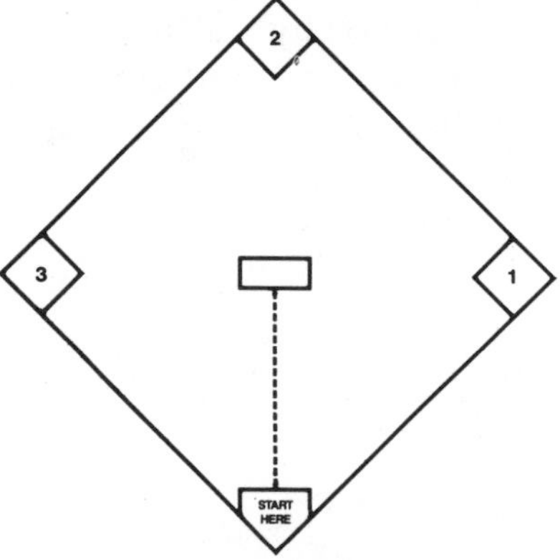

Its time now to measure your progress. Which of the statements on the facing page are true and which are false?

READING REVIEW

Answer the following true/false questions.

TRUE FALSE

_____ _____ 1. Team leaders emphasize each member's involvement and expect that person to take responsibility for his/her contributions.

_____ _____ 2. If you plan to build a strong team and use member's skills to the maximum, there is little need to improve your own skills.

_____ _____ 3. People are more productive when they feel a sense of ownership of the task or of the organization.

_____ _____ 4. When a true team achieves success, so will all of its' members.

_____ _____ 5. Selecting qualified people who work well with others at the outset, supports team building.

_____ _____ 6. Commitment to task accomplishment is the result when a leader involves team members in planning, goal setting and problem solving.

_____ _____ 7. Team leaders facilitate training for team members and coach them to apply what has been learned.

_____ _____ 8. Teams are more concerned with getting positive results than they are with ''turf'' considerations.

_____ _____ 9. Trust is a minor factor in most team situations.

_____ _____ 10. Team members need to know anything that affects the work they are performing.

_____ _____ 11. Competition and conflict in a team is healthy if it is properly controlled and quickly resolved.

_____ _____ 12. Open communication in a team will promote understanding, a recognition of individual differences and encourage mutual support.

_____ _____ 13. Teams participate in decision making but recognize their leader must act on his or her own if a consensus cannot be reached or there is a crisis.

_____ _____ 14. Successful teams have little need for recognition and praise.

_____ _____ 15. Self-control and good discipline are by-products of team building.

Check your answers with the author's on the next page.

READING REVIEW ANSWERS

1. True. Involvement and responsibility are critical to teams.
2. False. This is one of the most challenging times ever for leaders.
3. True. Ownership builds commitment and responsibility.
4. True. Success indicates everyone played their role.
5. True. Good people are the foundation for success.
6. True. You can't demand it or force it.
7. True. Leaders make training useful.
8. True. Productivity, commitment, open communication and trust are the usual casualties of "turf" wars.
9. False. Trust is one of the most vital ingredients.
10. True. The right information makes the job easier.
11. True. It is stimulating and mind opening.
12. True. Forget this principle at your own risk.
13. True. Timeliness is also important in decision making.
14. False. Recognition and praise are among the strongest motivators known.
15. True. People who are committed to a task, a unit and each other are not apt to create unnecessary problems.

TEN UNFORGIVABLE MISTAKES

Don't get trapped by the ten unforgivable mistakes listed on the next page.

DANGER AHEAD

TEN UNFORGIVABLE MISTAKES

Check ☑ those you intend to avoid.

- ☐ 1. Failure to develop and maintain basic management and leadership skills.
- ☐ 2. Permitting poor employee selection techniques.
- ☐ 3. Failure to discuss expectations or establish goals which have been mutually set.
- ☐ 4. Inattention to the training and development needs of team members.
- ☐ 5. Failure to advocate, support and nuture team building activities.
- ☐ 6. Preventing the involvement of team members in any activity where they could make a contribution.
- ☐ 7. Failure to provide and receive feedback from the team.
- ☐ 8. Allowing conflict and competition to get out of control, or trying to eliminate it altogether.
- ☐ 9. Depending on someone else to recognize and reward the team and its' members.
- ☐ 10. Failure to send players who have not responded to coaching back to the minor leagues.

REFLECT FOR A MOMENT ON WHAT YOU HAVE LEARNED–THEN DEVELOP A PERSONAL ACTION PLAN USING THE GUIDE ON THE NEXT PAGE.

DEVELOP A PERSONAL ACTION PLAN

Think over the material you have read. Review the self-analysis questionnaires. Re-think the case studies and the reinforcement exercises. What have you learned about team building? What did you learn about yourself? How can you apply what you learned? Make a commitment to yourself to become a better team player and a more effective team builder by designing a personal action plan to help you accomplish this goal.

The following guide may help you clarify your goals and outline actions required to achieve your goals.

1. My current team building skills are effective in the following areas:

   ____

   ____

   ____

2. I need to improve my team building skills in the following areas:

   ____

   ____

   ____

3. My goals for improving my team building skills are as follows:
   (Be sure they are specific, attainable and measurable.)

   ____

   ____

   ____

4. These people and resources can help me achieve my goals.

   ____

   ____

5. Following are my action steps, along with a time-table to accomplish each goal.

   ____

   ____

   ____

VOLUNTARY CONTRACT

Sometimes our desire to improve personal skills can be re-enforced by making a contract with a friend, spouse, or supervisor. If you believe a contract would help you, use the form on the following page.

VOLUNTARY

CONTRACT*

I, ______________________________ , hereby agree
(Your Name)
to meet with the individual designated below within thirty days to discuss my progress toward incorporating the techniques and ideas of team building. The purpose of this meeting will be to *review* areas of strength and establish action steps for areas where improvement may still be required.

____
Signature

I agree to meet with the above individual on

____
Month *Date* *Time*

at the following location.

____

____
Signature

*The purpose of this agreement is to motivate you to incorporate concepts and techniques of this program into your daily activities. It also provides a degree of accountability between you and your employer.

ANSWERS TO CASES

CASE 1—CAN THIS SUPERVISOR BE SAVED?

Mary Lou is in serious trouble. It will take real effort to turn things around. It appears Mary Lou is trapped by her office and her paperwork. She needs training to develop better competence and more confidence as a supervisor. Until Mary Lou learns to manage herself, she will be unable to manage anyone else. Her employees also seem untrained, unsure of themselves and poorly disciplined. Until they understand their jobs better and recognize the importance of cooperating with each other, chaos will be the result.

Since Mary Lou's group is interdependent it must work as a team to be successful. Mary Lou must try her best to learn and apply team concepts. Specifically, she must become a better leader and supervisor; build the skills and confidence of her employees; establish a better working climate; and institute an appropriate reward system. How to accomplish this is the basis for this book.

CASE 2—WHICH SUPERVISOR WOULD YOU PREFER?

It is good that both Morgana and Jeff recognize the importance of clear goals and plans. Employees who have limited knowledge or expertise may appreciate Morgana's approach because they have a great deal to learn. As they learn under Morgana's management however they may feel too restricted to share their ideas. New methods, better products and simpler ways to achieve objectives might not be forthcoming. Experienced employees may feel that way at the outset.

Experienced employees will appreciate Jeff's approach because it provides a needed outlet to contribute. They will feel free to improve the effectiveness of the group while improving their own. Employees with lesser skills will be encouraged to learn so they too can become more productive and contribute. Jeff's employees will appreciate his decision to participate in supervisory training because they appreciate a manager who knows the basics.

ANSWERS TO CASES (Continued)

CASE 3—THE COMPLAINING EMPLOYEES

Joyce and Sue have good reasons to complain. Joyce wants the opportunity to grow beyond her current tasks. Her efforts to learn what is expected of her have been blocked, and she is discouraged by waiting for assignments. She has been told not to worry about being idle and counseled not to help others unless directed to do so. This is frustrating for people who want to contribute.

Sue is suffering the consequences of poor communication from her supervisor. This is an impossible situation for Sue to correct until Janice either opens communication channels between users and Sue; or begins relaying information in a timely manner.

Janice appears to be over-controlling her employees by assuming they cannot think for themselves. She is also preventing voluntary attempts by employees to help and support one another. Janice needs to re-evaluate her approach to supervision and be more open in her dealings with employees. Otherwise Janice will soon be an ''ex-manager''.

CASE 4—RESOLVING CONFLICT

Using a win/lose approach (item 1) takes a problem solving opportunity away from Ginny and Jeremy and makes one of them a loser. Avoidance (item 2) leaves two recommendations unresolved. Accomodation (item 3) may work, but could be confusing to the operating department. Compromising (item 4) might be the best solution in this instance because it requires each employee to carefully examine his or her thinking in light of the other's arguments, and work together to reach an agreeable decision. During this process, they may end up using item 5, problem solving, because it not only gets the job done, it also satisfies the recommendation each made originally.

ABOUT THE FIFTY-MINUTE SERIES

"Fifty-Minute books are the best new publishing idea in years. They are clear, practical, concise and affordable — perfect for today's world."

Leo Hauser
(Past President, ASTD)

What Is A Fifty-Minute Book?

—Fifty-Minute books are brief, soft-cover, "self-study" modules which cover a single concept. They are reasonably priced, and ideal for formal training programs, excellent for self-study and perfect for remote location training.

Why Are Fifty-Minute Books Unique?

—Because of their format and level. Designed to be "read with a pencil," the basics of a subject can be quickly grasped and applied through a series of hands-on activities, exercises and cases.

How Many Fifty-Minute Books Are There?

—Those listed on the facing page at this time, however, additional titles are in development. For more information write to **Crisp Publications, Inc., 95 First Street, Los Altos, CA 94022.**

Crisp books are distributed in Canada by Reid Publishing, Ltd., P.O. Box 7267, Oakville, Ontario, Canada L6J 6L6.

In Australia by Career Builders, P.O. Box 1051 Springwood, Brisbane, Queensland, Australia 4127.

And in New Zealand by Career Builders, P.O. Box 571, Manurewa, New Zealand.

THE FIFTY-MINUTE SERIES

Quantity	Title	Code #	Price	Amount
	The Fifty-Minute Supervisor—*2nd Edition*	58-0	$6.95	
	Effective Performance Appraisals—*Revised*	11-4	$6.95	
	Successful Negotiation—*Revised*	09-2	$6.95	
	Quality Interviewing—*Revised*	13-0	$6.95	
	Team Building: An Exercise in Leadership—*Revised*	16-5	$7.95	
	Performance Contracts: The Key To Job Success—*Revised*	12-2	$6.95	
	Personal Time Management	22-X	$6.95	
	Effective Presentation Skills	24-6	$6.95	
	Better Business Writing	25-4	$6.95	
	Quality Customer Service	17-3	$6.95	
	Telephone Courtesy & Customer Service	18-1	$6.95	
	Restaurant Server's Guide To Quality Service—*Revised*	08-4	$6.95	
	Sales Training Basics—*Revised*	02-5	$6.95	
	Personal Counseling—*Revised*	14-9	$6.95	
	Balancing Home & Career	10-6	$6.95	
	Mental Fitness: A Guide To Emotional Health	15-7	$6.95	
	Attitude: Your Most Priceless Possession	21-1	$6.95	
	Preventing Job Burnout	23-8	$6.95	
	Successful Self-Management	26-2	$6.95	
	Personal Financial Fitness	20-3	$7.95	
	Job Performance and Chemical Dependency	27-0	$7.95	
	Career Discovery—*Revised*	07-6	$6.95	
	Study Skills Strategies—*Revised*	05-X	$6.95	
	I Got The Job!—*Revised*	59-9	$6.95	
	Effective Meetings Skills	33-5	$7.95	
	The Business of Listening	34-3	$6.95	
	Professional Sales Training	42-4	$7.95	
	Customer Satisfaction: The Other Half of Your Job	57-2	$7.95	
	Managing Disagreement Constructively	41-6	$7.95	
	Professional Excellence for Secretaries	52-1	$6.95	
	Starting A Small Business: A Resource Guide	44-0	$7.95	
	Developing Positive Assertiveness	38-6	$6.95	
	Writing Fitness-Practical Exercises for Better Business Writing	35-1	$7.95	
	An Honest Day's Work: Motivating Employees to Give Their Best	39-4	$6.95	
	Marketing Your Consulting & Professional Services	40-8	$7.95	
	Time Management On The Telephone	53-X	$6.95	
	Training Managers to Train	43-2	$7.95	
	New Employee Orientation	46-7	$6.95	
	The Art of Communicating: Achieving Impact in Business	45-9	$7.95	
	Technical Presentation Skills	55-6	$7.95	
	Plan B: Protecting Your Career from the Winds of Change	48-3	$7.95	
	A Guide To Affirmative Action	54-8	$7.95	
	Memory Skills in Business	56-4	$6.95	

(Continued on next page)

THE FIFTY-MINUTE SERIES
(Continued)

☐ Send volume discount information.

☐ Add my name to CPI's mailing list.

	Amount
Total (from other side)	
Shipping ($1.50 first book, $.50 per title thereafter)	
California Residents add 7% tax	
Total	

Ship to: ______________________________

____

____

____

Phone number: ______________________________

Bill to: ______________________________

____

____

____

P.O. # ______________________________

All orders except those with a P.O.# must be prepaid.
Call (415) 949-4888 for more information.

NO POSTAGE NECESSARY IF MAILED IN THE UNITED STATES

BUSINESS REPLY
FIRST CLASS PERMIT NO. 884 LOS ALTOS, CA

POSTAGE WILL BE PAID BY ADDRESSEE

Crisp Publications, Inc.
95 First Street
Los Altos, CA 94022